# What Is the Impact of
# DECLINING
# BIODIVERSITY?

## Other titles in the *Environmental Impact* series include:

What Is the Impact of Climate Change?
What Is the Impact of Excessive Waste and Garbage?
What Is the Impact of Ocean Pollution?

# *Environmental* IMPACT

# *What Is the Impact of*
# DECLINING
# BIODIVERSITY?

**Stuart A. Kallen**

ReferencePoint Press®

San Diego, CA

**For more information, contact:**
ReferencePoint Press, Inc.
PO Box 27779
San Diego, CA 92198
www.ReferencePointPress.com

LIBRARY OF CONGRESS CATALOGING-IN-PUBLICATION DATA

Names: Kallen, Stuart A., 1955- author.
Title: What is the impact of declining biodiversity? / Stuart A. Kallen.
Description: San Diego, CA : ReferencePoint Press, 2021. | Series:
   Environmental impact | Includes bibliographical references and index.
Identifiers: LCCN 2020001456 (print) | LCCN 2020001457 (ebook) | ISBN
   9781682828618 (library binding) | ISBN 9781682828625 (ebook)
Subjects: LCSH: Biodiversity conservation--Juvenile literature. |
   Biodiversity--Juvenile literature. | Biotic communities--Environmental
   aspects--Juvenile literature. | Population--Environmental
   aspects--Juvenile literature.
Classification: LCC QH75 .K337 2021  (print) | LCC QH75  (ebook) | DDC
   333.95/16--dc23
LC record available at https://lccn.loc.gov/2020001456
LC ebook record available at https://lccn.loc.gov/2020001457

# Contents

# The War on Nature

In 2019 there were about 7.7 billion humans on Earth, more than double the number of people alive in 1969. During that fifty-year period, the impact of humanity on the natural environment increased proportionately. According to a hard-hitting 2019 United Nations report by the Intergovernmental Science-Policy Platform on Biodiversity and Ecosystem Services (IPBES), 75 percent of Earth's land surface has been significantly altered by farming, logging, mining, oil extraction, building, and other human activities. Two-thirds of the world's major rivers have been dammed and disrupted, and 85 percent of wetlands have been lost to development. Carbon dioxide emitted by fossil fuel–burning vehicles, factories, and power plants is altering the climate and changing the chemistry of the oceans.

The influence of civilization on nature has been so profound that Nobel Prize–winning chemist Paul J. Crutzen invented the term *Anthropocene* in 2002 to describe this new era. The Anthropocene, or human-influenced, epoch is defined by the way people are altering the composition of the air, land, water, and atmosphere. These changes, which have rapidly accelerated since the early 1900s, will continue to affect all life on Earth for thousands of years to come. Previous geological epochs were defined by natural forces such as volcanic eruptions, shifting continents, and even meteorite strikes. For example, it is believed that dinosaurs were wiped out at the end of the Late Cretaceous epoch around 66 million years ago when a large meteorite collided with Earth, causing the climate to cool rapidly. But for the first time in Earth's geological history, human beings are at the center of epochal change. Crutzen and journalist Christian Schwägerl assert, "By cutting down rainforests, moving mountains to access coal deposits and acidifying coral reefs, we fundamentally change the biology and the geology of the planet. While driving uncountable numbers of species to extinction, we . . . [build] our man-made ecosystems, including 'mega-regions' with more than 100 million inhabitants."[1]

## Loss of Biodiversity

All this human activity is causing a loss of biodiversity—the diversity of plant, animal, algae, fungi, and microbe species in a given environment, including the planet as a whole. But the survival of humanity—and all life on Earth—is directly related to biodiversity. The wide variety of species present in nature is vital for global food production and clean air and water. Bees, butterflies, bats, birds, and other animals are essential for pollinating seventy-one of the one hundred plants that make up most of the world's food supply. Despite their importance, pollinators, which have thrived for millions of years, are facing extinction in startling numbers. In North America alone, billions of birds representing hundreds of species have died out since the late 1960s due to pesticide use and loss of habitat.

> ### IMPACT FACTS
> Around 80 percent of all flowering plant species are pollinated by bees, butterflies, bats, birds, and other wild animals.
>
> —Food and Agriculture Organization of the United Nations

While providing humanity with food, biodiversity also helps slow the effects of climate change. Mature forests capture and store the carbon dioxide generated by human activities, which is a process called carbon sequestration. Eighty percent of the world's land-based species depend on forests to live, but forests around the world are under threat. This problem is particularly acute in the Amazon rain forest in South America, where forests are being logged, burned, and converted into cattle ranches at a rate that has accelerated since 2018. This is causing the decline of countless species of plants, insects, and animals. And scientists have no idea exactly how many species live in the Amazon.

The Amazon River and other waterways, as well as the world's oceans, are also important for the survival of humans and other life-forms. Nearly half of Earth's population relies on fish and other seafood as a major source of protein. But warming oceans, acidification, and plastic pollution are threatening numerous fish species along with marine mammals, kelp forests, and coral reefs.

In 2011 an extensive ten-year, $650 million study was conducted by a scientific organization called the Census of Marine Life. The study determined that approximately 8.7 million species exist on Earth; around 6.5 million live on land, and 2.2 million can be found in the oceans. But only 1.7 million species have been studied. According to lead author of the study Camilo Mora, "The question of how many species exist . . . is particularly important

Wetlands, such as this one in northwestern Canada's Yukon Territory, are biologically diverse environments. Sadly, 85 percent of the world's wetlands have been lost due to human activities such as farming and construction.

now because a host of human activities and influences are accelerating the rate of extinctions. Many species may vanish before we even know of their existence, of their unique niche and function in ecosystems, and of their potential contribution to improved human well-being."[2]

Although climate change receives widespread attention from governments, the problems associated with declining biodiversity are low on the political agenda. Compared to climate summits, few heads of state attend biodiversity talks held by the United Nations and other organizations. The problem, however, is just as urgent. The IPBES says 1 million species of flora and fauna are at risk of extinction within decades. This will be the worst loss of life on Earth since the demise of the dinosaurs. As Swedish climate activist Greta Thunberg insists, "The war against nature must end."[3] The challenge is to transform humanity's long-established farming, fishing, and manufacturing methods into sustainable practices that benefit or at least do not damage the planet's biodiversity.

# Chapter One

# What Is Biodiversity?

Paul R. Ehrlich is a conservation researcher. Ehrlich encourages people to think of each species as one of the rivets that secures a wing to an airplane. If one rivet pops out, the wing will hold together and the plane will safely fly through the air. But if too many rivets pop out, the plane will crash. In 2009 Ehrlich explained the rivet-popping theory as it applies to biodiversity: "Even though you don't know the value of each [species], you know it's nuttier than hell to keep removing them. There is some redundancy, but we don't know how much. And facing serious climate disruption, humanity is going to need more redundancy in the little rivets, the species and populations that run the world."[4]

All species, even those that are unknown or little studied, play an important role in the biodiversity of nature. When these species disappear, humanity can suffer. One example is the spread of a rare disease called hantavirus, which, in humans, causes intense headaches, fever, kidney failure, and death. Hantavirus was unknown in the United States until 1993. Since that time, the disease has infected more than 730 people in thirty-six states and killed at least 250. Hantavirus is spread by mice and rats. Ehrlich believes that a lack of biodiversity is responsible for these fatalities:

What difference does it make if we put a strip mall in here and . . . this little mouse goes extinct? . . . It turns out that if you reduce the diversity of the different species of rodents . . . in a forest, the rodents that carry hantaviruses can become more common. And the results for human beings are more death and disease. So by reducing the diversity of mouse-like creatures in a forest, you can make that forest more dangerous for people.[5]

## Ancient Forests

Humans are one of millions of species that make up the biosphere, the name given to all the various ecosystems of the natural world. All species alive today evolved to develop unique traits that allow them to survive in their environment, whether it be a forest, ocean, lake, grassland, tundra, or desert. Every species in the biosphere depends on other species to survive. As biologist Rachel Carson wrote in 1962, "In nature nothing exists alone."[6] The connectedness of all species is often referred to as the web of life.

This wood mouse is just one of many rodent species in the forest. Some rodents spread diseases such as hantaviruses to humans. Reducing the diversity of rodent species can lead to an increase in the number of rodents that carry and spread these diseases.

Earth is estimated to be around 4.5 billion years old, and the biosphere has evolved continually during that time. It is estimated that more than 5 billion species have lived on Earth at one time or another, and 99.9 percent of them are now extinct. Today, the millions of species that live on Earth are unevenly distributed. Tropical forests located in Central and South America, Africa, and elsewhere contain 90 percent of the world's species. Though they cover only 10 percent of Earth's surface, these warm, wet environments that exist along the equator provide an ideal environment for biodiversity.

**IMPACT FACTS**

An estimated 5 billion species have inhabited Earth over the past 4.5 billion years—99.9 percent of them are now extinct.

—Daniel Simberloff, professor of environmental studies

No one knows exactly why equatorial areas are home to the greatest number of species, but researchers have theories. One of the most prevalent of these theories focuses on the climate along the equator. While it is typically hot, temperatures are relatively stable. Most tropical species cannot survive in cold temperatures. With a warm year-round growing season, tropical plants reproduce much faster. This allows them to evolve more quickly than plants that are dormant during the winter in colder regions. Additionally, the ecosystems found in tropical rain forests are very old; forests like those found in the Amazon have existed for many millions of years and once covered the entire planet. This extended timeline provided a very long period during which birds, mammals, insects, trees, and other species were able to diversify. By contrast, most of Canada and the northern United States was covered with a mile-thick (1.6 km) sheet of ice as recently as twenty thousand years ago. That means that the forests growing in Ontario, Quebec, Maine, and parts of northern Ohio and New York have only been evolving for several thousands of years. This explains why the boreal forests of Canada, which make up 25 percent of all intact forests on Earth, contain only twenty tree species, compared to over one thousand in the Amazon.

## Biodiversity Hot Spots

Areas that host the largest variety of species are known as biodiversity hot spots. To qualify as a biodiversity hot spot, an ecosystem must contain at least fifteen hundred endemic species—those that are found in only one particular location. Manú National Park, located in the Amazon rain forest in southeastern Peru, is one such biodiversity hot spot. The elevation of the sprawling reserve in the Andes Mountains rises from about 1,150 feet above sea level to over 13,000 feet (351 to 3,962 m). The park encompasses several distinct ecosystems, including high mountain grasslands, rain forests, and damp, mossy cloud forests that are often enveloped in low-level clouds. The immense variety of altitudes, soils, and other ecological conditions makes Manú National Park "possibly the most biologically diverse protected area in the world,"[7] according to the United Nations.

Manú has more than one thousand species of trees. The park is home to eight hundred bird species—one of every nine bird species on Earth. Scientists estimate that there are more than two

*A scarlet macaw flies through the palm trees in Peru's Manú National Park. Scientists estimate that the park is home to eight hundred species of birds and more than two hundred species of mammals.*

hundred species of mammals in the park, including thirteen differ-ent primate species and eight species of big cat, such as jaguars, pumas, and the endangered Andean mountain cat. Manú also is home to numerous endemic species, including a bird called the white-cheeked tody-flycatcher and a tiny black toad with the Latin name *Rhinella manu.*

In addition to providing habitat for countless species, Manú National Park has important research value, according to the United Nations Educational, Scientific and Cultural Organization:

> For decades, the property has been among the foremost references for scientific research in tropical ecology. As such the property has significantly helped our under-standing of tropical forest ecosystems. Even seasoned researchers are overwhelmed not only by the diversity of life but also by the impressive abundance of verte-brates, including mammals. Despite the major record of research, even today . . . studies invariably reveal spe-cies unknown to science, including vertebrates, clear evidence that Manú continues to hold many of its biodi-versity secrets.[8]

## Biodiversity in the Soil

Although rain forest biodiversity receives a great deal of atten-tion from scientists and environmentalists, the most biologically diverse ecosystem on the planet is its soil. The planet's soil hosts a web of biological activity that plays a critically important role for all life on Earth. Each region's soil differs depending on local veg-etation, rainfall, and other environmental factors, but whether that soil is in a dense forest or on an arid mountaintop, it is made up of minerals, liquids, gases, fungi, bacteria, and other organic matter. Soil helps modify the atmosphere and stores and purifies water. It provides a medium for plants to grow in and acts as a habitat for insects and other organisms.

## Threats to Manú National Park

Manú National Park is a biodiversity hot spot in Peru that is valued for its natural wonders. But the park's biodiversity is facing threats from a number of sources. Gas companies plan to drill for oil along the park's borderlands. Illegal loggers have clear-cut forests, destroying natural habitats for some of the endemic species in the park. Drug traffickers cut down trees to plant coca, which is refined into cocaine. Perhaps the biggest threat comes from gold miners who have destroyed over 370,000 acres (149,734 ha) of Amazon rain forest in Brazil, located along the park's western border. Miners dig into the earth for gold, using the toxic metal mercury to leach tiny pieces of gold out of the soil. When the gold is removed, the mercury is dumped into waterways. This poisons fish stocks and pollutes the water supplies relied on by the indigenous Mashco-Piro people. Environmental activist Nilo D'Avila calls the gold mining an epidemic: "We are talking about impact on biodiversity and forests, we are talking about the use of mercury, we are talking about stealing [resources] from indigenous people."

Quoted in Dom Phillips, "Illegal Mining in Amazon Rainforest Has Become an 'Epidemic,'" *The Guardian*, December 10, 2018. www.theguardian.com.

Scientists call the entirety of Earth's soil the pedosphere. Only 1 percent of the species in this broadly diverse ecosystem have been classified. Still, biologists divide the biodiversity of the pedosphere into three broad categories: microfauna, mesofauna, and macrofauna. The microfauna category includes microbes and microscopic animals with body widths of less than 100 micrometers, or 0.1 millimeters (0.004 in). The mesofauna category comprises animals with body widths between 100 micrometers and 2 millimeters (0.08 in), and the macrofauna includes those larger than 2 millimeters.

Soil macrofauna includes familiar creatures like termites, earthworms, beetles, and spiders. The term also applies to mushrooms and other larger fungi. Some species of tiny insects, such as mites, springtails, and insect larvae, are considered mesofauna. The microfauna category includes 1 million species of microscopic organisms called nematodes, or roundworms. About 60 billion nematodes exist for every human on Earth, and these simple life-forms can be found everywhere—from the equator to the polar regions, and from mountaintops to the deepest mines ever tunneled beneath the ground. They even live in the ocean.

## The "Wood-Wide Web"

Because it is underfoot, soil biodiversity is often underappreciated or overlooked. But plants and soils are intricately linked in a cycle of dependence known as plant-soil feedback. Plant-soil feedback occurs when plants alter the properties of the soil, which in turn influences the health of plants. Plants capture critically important nutrients such as nitrogen and phosphorus from biodiverse soil networks created by fungus, bacteria, and nematodes. When plants shed dead leaves or flowers, or die themselves, they return these nutrients to the soil as they decompose. This enriches the soil for the next generation of plants, feeding seeds as they grow into seedlings and mature plants.

A substantial body of scientific evidence shows that that plant-soil feedback also allows trees of the same species to communicate with one another. This is done through what are called mycorrhizal networks. These networks consist of microscopic fungal filaments that live underground on the fine root hairs of trees. The mycorrhizal networks connect trees so they can share water and nutrients. The networks also allow trees to send distress signals to other trees about drought, disease, or insect attacks. Trees that receive the messages can alter their behavior by retaining water or building up chemicals that repel insects. German forester Peter Wohlleben calls mycorrhizal networks the "wood-wide web."[9]

The fungi in this network have extremely thin filaments that weave through the ground in an astonishing density. A single teaspoon of forest soil contains fungal filaments that range from single cells to chains of cells that can stretch for several miles. And a single fungus can cover many square miles while supporting an entire forest network. (Mushrooms are the fruit of the network; they pop up and spread spores to help it reproduce.) This highly evolved type of biodiversity is quickly destroyed when large trees are logged. The underground networks are also damaged by forest fires.

Soil biodiversity can become extremely specialized, as researchers in the Pacific rain forests of British Columbia have discovered. Scientists found a type of fungus that had a chemical fingerprint showing that it absorbed nitrogen from salmon. As researcher Allen Larocque explains, "We know that bears sit under trees and eat salmon, and leave the carcasses there. What we're finding is that trees are absorbing salmon nitrogen, and

## Burning Biodiversity

When forest fires occur, the aboveground effects, such as the charred remains of trees, are easily observed. But researchers are learning that fires also damage the biodiversity of underground fungal communities. In 2014 a destructive wildfire burned a record 7 million acres (2.8 million ha) of boreal pine forest in Canada's Northwest Territory. The following year scientists studied the soil and found that mushrooms and the mycorrhizal fungi network that grows on tree roots were much less abundant.

Fires are a natural occurrence in boreal forests. The flames clear away dead brush and allow sun to reach seedlings on the forest floor. Some species in the soil ecosystem even thrive after a fire. Morel mushrooms, which are valued by gourmet cooks, prefer the chemistry of burnt soil and spring up in large numbers after a burn. But the hotter, drier summers caused by climate change are causing forests to burn at much hotter temperatures than they have in the past. This is causing an overall decline in belowground biodiversity that will determine long-term growth patterns of forests after they burn.

then sharing it with each other through the [mycorrhizal] network. It's an interlinked system: fish-forest-fungi."[10]

## Disturbing the Soil

The loss of soil biodiversity is a serious issue almost everywhere. When natural land is paved or plowed, soil fauna is affected along with the plants that once grew on it. This loss of biodiversity in the soil leaves important food crops, such as wheat, corn, rice, potatoes, and soybeans, susceptible to pests and diseases. This prompts farmers to use more pesticides and herbicides, which kill almost all natural soil fauna. As a result, in many places where crops are grown, the soil is lifeless; farmers thus have to apply synthetic fertilizers to grow crops in this soil that lacks natural nutrients. Wohlleben writes, "When we step into farm fields, the vegetation becomes very quiet. Thanks to selective breeding, our cultivated plants have, for the most part, lost their ability to communicate above or below ground—you could say they are deaf and dumb."[11]

## The Biological Desert Crust

When soil biodiversity is disturbed, it can impact human health, especially in desert regions. Although desert soil might look barren, it is actually teaming with stress-resistant bacteria and microscopic fungi that thrive in extreme environments. These microbes root themselves onto grains of sand, weaving together a surface called a biological desert crust. The soil in the crusted desert surfaces can resist hurricane-force winds without blowing into the air. The microbes also provide nutrients to desert plants such as agave and cacti.

Desert microbes are extremely tough and can survive with little water in extreme temperatures. But when they are trampled by cattle or people, squashed under vehicle tires, or scraped by bulldozers, the microbes lose their grip. They dry out quickly and die. It can take decades for the microbe network to recover, and in many places it never does.

Haboob dust storms, like this one in the Arizona desert, combine heavy rain, thunder and lightning, and powerful winds. These storms carry dust as well as microbes containing plant and animal viruses and other pathogens, sometimes hundreds of miles.

When the biological desert crust is destroyed, severe dust storms and sandstorms follow. Residents of Phoenix, Arizona, are familiar with massive dust storms referred to by the Arabic word *haboob*, which means "strong wind." Haboobs are massive storms that combine dust, heavy rain, thunder and lightning, and winds that can reach 70 miles per hour (113 kmh). Haboobs develop quickly and can engulf an entire city. While the dust storms have long occurred over the Sahara Desert in Africa, they are a recent phenomenon in Phoenix, where large areas of the biological desert crust have been destroyed due to unchecked development. In addition to bringing vehicle and air traffic to a halt, haboobs are unhealthy. The storms carry dust, which irritates the eyes and respiratory system, along with billions of microbes that contain plant and animal viruses and other pathogenic organisms. And these harmful microbes can be carried hundreds of miles from the dust storms' origins. For example, microbes from the Sahara have been found in the snows of the Alps Mountains in Switzerland.

## The Value of Ecosystems

Soil microbes, rain forest flowers, boreal pines, and countless other species have inhabited Earth for millions of years. The human species, *Homo sapiens*, is a relative newcomer, having evolved in Africa around 350,000 years ago. While *Homo sapiens* have never been as strong or as fertile as other species, they quickly developed the unique ability among animals to drastically reshape the environment. Humans cut down forests, level mountains, plow up grasslands, and move plants and animals from one continent to another. Although this dominance has allowed humanity to grow and thrive, the fate of *Homo sapiens* is intertwined with the biodiversity of the Earth. As Ehrlich explains,

> The human economy is a wholly owned subsidiary of the economy of nature, which supplies us . . . [with] what are called 'ecosystem services'—keeping carbon dioxide out of the atmosphere, supplying fresh water, preventing floods, protecting our crops from pests and pollinating many of them, recycling the nutrients that are essential to agriculture and forestry, and on and on.[12]

Without biodiversity there are no ecosystem services, no *Homo sapiens*, and no life anywhere on Earth.

# Chapter Two

# Hostile Invaders

The United States is home to sixty national parks, including Yosemite, Yellowstone, Grand Canyon, Great Smoky Mountains, and the Everglades. These parks are natural wonders with breathtaking scenery, historic and cultural artifacts, and wildlife found nowhere else on Earth. Americans love their parks; in 2018 national parks and monuments, recreation areas, and other park reserves were visited by over 318 million people.

Humans are not the only creatures who love the national parks. A 2019 study by the journal *Biological Invasions* found that more than half of the national parks in the United States are threatened by invasive plant, animal, and insect species. These intrusive creatures, sometimes called bio-invaders, spread disease, compete for food, prey on native species, and alter the natural environment. The most destructive invasive species are also the most commonplace. As Ashley Dayer, the author of the *Biological Invasions* study, explains,

Invasive rats, cats, and mosquitoes carrying disease have caused the extinction of endemic island birds in the Pacific, such as Hawaii. There and throughout much of the U.S., feral hogs destroy wildlife habitat impacting birds and small mammals. Likewise, feral cats are considered to be among the most destructive invasive species globally for their predation of birds and other animals.[13]

## Feral Cats

Humans might be considered the most invasive species on Earth. Since the seventeenth century, *Homo sapiens* have traveled to every remote area of the globe and have upset delicate ecosystems along the way. But humans do not travel alone; they also transport dogs, cats, and other domestic animals such as cows, pigs, sheep, and goats. Pests like rats, fleas, and mosquitoes also travel wherever humans go, inadvertently carried to new environments in ships and other vessels. All of these nonnative invaders have seriously damaged biodiversity in fragile ecosystems.

Feral cats, which are the same species as house cats, live, hunt, and breed in the wild. These cats have followed humans in their travels for thousands of years. According to the Humane Society, there are around 40 million feral cats in the United States and millions more around the world. The International Union for

*A feral cat walks across hardened lava in Hawaii. Feral cats are found on all eight islands of Hawaii and are considered one of the main threats to biodiversity in the state.*

Conservation of Nature lists cats among the world's top 100 most invasive species. In most places, feral cats are descendants of house cats that were abandoned or purposely let loose to control rat populations. But cats are exceptional hunters that will eat almost anything, including birds, amphibians, reptiles, and small mammals.

Feral cats are particularly destructive on islands. They are found on all eight islands of Hawaii and are considered one of the main threats to biodiversity in the state. Islands throughout the world are home to around half of the world's endangered species, and feral cats are responsible for an estimated 14 percent of all extinctions in these isolated environments. In one example, a single female cat on a small island south of New Zealand caused the extinction of the Stephens Island wren, a small flightless bird found nowhere else in the world.

**IMPACT FACTS**

There are around 40 million feral cats in the United States.

—Humane Society

Most island species do not have natural defenses against predators like cats. A single feral cat can kill fifty to sixty birds a month. And birds are extremely important to the biodiversity of an environment. They pollinate plants, spread seeds, and eat large numbers of insects. Large populations of birds are an indicator of a healthy ecosystem.

## Monster Kudzu

Like most invasive species, feral cats reproduce fast and quickly spread through the environment. Invasive plants can also follow this pattern. A leafy vine called kudzu exemplifies the problem. Kudzu, a member of the pea family, is native to India, China, and Japan. Kudzu, which has grape-scented flowers that produce purple honey, was originally brought to the United States as a decorative plant during the late nineteenth century. The plant might have remained an obscure novelty if not for the damaging dust storms that swept across the prairies of Kansas, Oklahoma,

Texas, and other parts of the Great Plains from 1934 to 1940. These massive storms of black, blowing dust were a result of biodiversity loss. The native plains grass species had deep roots, which retained moisture and held the soil in place. In the early twentieth century, farmers plowed the native grasses under and replaced them with corn. The dirt dried up and blew into the sky, turning the Great Plains into the Dust Bowl.

Searching for a solution to the dust storms, a federal agency called the Soil Conservation Service turned to kudzu as a way to control soil erosion. The service paid nurseries to grow 70 million kudzu seedlings and offered farmers what was then the large sum of eight dollars an acre to plant the fast-growing vine. Although the vine was unsuitable for the arid Great Plains, farmers in southern states were happy to cash the government checks and plant the vines. Loggers, railroad builders, and highway developers were also looking for a plant that would cover the erosive gashes their labors created.

## IMPACT FACTS

There are around 5 million feral pigs in the United States.

—US Department of Agriculture

When the government stopped paying farmers to plant kudzu in 1945, most farmers plowed the plant under. But the untended plantings by roadsides, railroad beds, and clear-cut forests thrived in the hot, humid southern climate. Horticulturist Bill Finch writes, "Those roadside plantings—isolated from grazing, impractical to manage, their shoots shimmying up the trunks of second-growth trees—looked like monsters. The miraculous vine that might have saved the South had become, in the eyes of many, a notorious vine bound to consume it."[14]

### A Suffocating Killer

By the early 1960s, kudzu was commonly referred to as the plant that ate the South. The plant can grow up to 2 feet (61 cm) a day, and it snakes up trees, telephone poles, and everything else in its way. Estimates of kudzu's spread vary widely. For example,

## Pig Problems

When Spanish explorer Hernando de Soto landed in Florida in 1539, his expedition included 620 soldiers and at least 200 pigs. The explorers released the pigs as they traveled through the southeast and hunted them for sport. During the nineteenth century, the feral descendants of those swine bred with European wild boars that were brought to the country for hunting. The crossbred animals are sometimes referred to as super pigs, and they have caused major damage to fragile ecosystems from Florida to California to Montana.

Feral pigs can weigh up to 700 pounds (318 kg), and their populations grow rapidly. Each female can have two litters a year of six or more piglets. The pigs spend their days rooting—digging up plants by the roots for food. They will eat anything, including crops, acorns, grasses, berries, roots, flower bulbs, worms, reptiles, ground-nesting birds, frogs, fish, small mammals, and even other pigs. Forests and fields are damaged by the rooting, which also destroys habitat that deer and other animals depend on. Rooting causes erosion; exposed dirt washes into streams along with pig manure, fouling waterways and threatening aquatic animals, including frogs and fish. Feral pigs spread at least thirty-two diseases—which can harm livestock and people—including bovine tuberculosis and *E. coli*. The pigs are big and nasty-tempered. They will attack with razor-sharp teeth when they feel threatened. In 2019 a fifty-nine-year-old woman in Texas was killed by a pack of feral pigs.

whereas the US Forest Service estimates that kudzu is spreading at a rate of 2,500 acres (1,012 ha) annually, the US Department of Agriculture says the vine is invading 150,000 acres (60,703 ha) per year. Whatever the exact figure, the vine is believed to blanket around 7.4 million acres (2.9 million ha) in southeastern states, including Mississippi, Tennessee, Alabama, Florida, Georgia, and North and South Carolina. Kudzu has been seen in Ohio, New Jersey, and even New York City. The vine has also invaded national parks, including the Great Smoky Mountains National Park.

The leafy kudzu suffocates everything below it, and the sheer weight of the plant can uproot mature trees. Kudzu destroys biodiversity by disrupting the food chain and threatening vegetation

Kudzu (pictured) is an invasive species that overtakes other vegetation and suffocates it. It destroys biodiversity by disrupting the food chain and threatening vegetation that native animals use for food and shelter.

that native animals use for food and shelter. The root systems drain water from the soil, and as kudzu decomposes it releases excessive carbon, increasing the threat of climate change.

Like many invasive species, the vine is a costly problem. The Forest Service estimates that kudzu causes an average of $300 million a year in lost forest productivity. The plant can be eliminated using highly toxic herbicides that contaminate the soil and carry suspected carcinogens. But killing the dense kudzu plant requires massive amounts of herbicides, costing farmers and utility companies about $5,000 an acre. Ironically, the biggest threat to kudzu seems to be from another invasive species: the Japanese kudzu beetle. This tiny beetle was first discovered in Atlanta, Georgia, in 2009. Millions of the bugs, which emit a foul odor when disturbed, cover kudzu leaves and suck the vital juices out of them, killing the plant. However, Japanese kudzu beetles also feed on soybeans, green beans, and other food crops. Biologists are worried that the invasive insect might spread beyond the kudzu stands, causing extensive damage to agricultural crops.

## Toxic Dispersal Machines

Like many invasive species, kudzu was introduced to solve one problem but created others. The cane toad was similarly seen as a solution to farmers' problems and has gone on to become one of the most invasive species anywhere on Earth. Cane toads, also known as bufo toads, are considered the giants of the amphibian world. Male toads can grow to be more than 9 inches (23 cm) long and weigh nearly 2 pounds (0.9 kg). The toads share survival features common to most invasive species: they are impervious to predators, they reproduce in astounding numbers, they live a long time, and they can eat almost anything. The warty skin of the cane toad produces toxins that sicken or kill most animals that try to eat it. A female cane toad lays thousands of eggs each year

**IMPACT FACTS**

The invasive vine kudzu causes an average of $300 million a year in lost forest productivity.

—US Forest Service

and lives for up to fifteen years in the wild and thirty-five years in captivity. The toad's diet consists of small rodents, reptiles, other frogs, and even birds and bats. They will also eat dog food, plants, and garbage.

Cane toads are native to Central and South America, where their numbers are kept in check by native predators, including fish, eels, snakes, and a type of crocodile called the broad-snouted caiman. The cane toad was introduced to several Caribbean islands, including Jamaica and Barbados, during the mid-nineteenth century in a failed attempt to control the rat population. During the early twentieth century, cane toads were brought to Puerto Rico by agricultural interests that hoped the toads would eat gray beetles that were damaging sugarcane crops. The plan worked. In this era before chemical insecticides were developed, cane toads were seen as a solution to the infestation problems farmers were

Invasive species have moved around the globe on ships for centuries. The bubonic plague, which wiped out about one-third of the European population during the fourteenth century, was caused by fleas carried by rats, which were in turn carried on ships traveling from Mongolia to Italy. Although the plague is no longer a threat, the number of bio-invaders hitching rides on ships is surging as global maritime trade increases.

Shipping accounts for 80 percent of world trade and has been responsible for transporting destructive marine invaders like green crabs, zebra mussels, and a strain of seaweed known as killer algae. Other bio-invaders, such as Asian gypsy moths, Asian tiger mosquitoes, and ship rats travel in pallets, shipping containers, and baggage holds. The problem is expected to grow, contends biologist Brian Leung:

> Biological invasions are believed to be a major driver of biodiversity change, and cause billions of dollars in economic damages annually. . . . Our models show that the emerging global shipping network could yield a three-fold to 20-fold increase in global marine invasion risk between now and 2050. . . . Unless appropriate action is taken, we could anticipate an exponential increase in such invasions, with potentially huge economic and ecological consequences.

As wealth and population increase throughout the world, the demand for shipped goods also grows. And Leung believes that shipping growth will outweigh climate change in the spread of invasive pests to new environments in coming decades.

Quoted in McGill University, "Rising Global Shipping Traffic Could Lead to Surge in Invasive Species: Maritime Trade Likely to Far Outweigh Climate Change as Driver of Bio-invasions over Next 30 Years, Study Finds," ScienceDaily, March 18, 2019. www.sciencedaily.com.

having in other parts of the world. During the 1930s, scientists released cane toads in a number of places to control gray beetles, including other Caribbean islands, Florida, the Philippines, parts of Japan, and Hawaii. When scientists began studying cane toads several decades later, they realized that populations had exploded and the amphibians were a much more serious pest than gray beetles. The toads were consuming native species of frogs, toads, snakes, and mammals. When dogs and cats, and even alligators, tried to eat them, they died.

The cane toad population explosion in Australia exemplified the problem. In 1935, 101 cane toads were released in the northeastern state of Queensland, followed by a release of 62,000 two years later. The toads rapidly reproduced, and scientists estimate that there are now anywhere from 200 million to 1.5 billion toxic toads in the country. Australian cane toads have evolved over the years, with longer back legs that enable them to travel great distances. Such evolutionary changes have allowed cane toads to expand their range to more than 1,200 miles (1,931 km) beyond Queensland. As biology professor Rick Shine explained in 2017, "The [toads] at the invasion front up in the tropics are moving often kilometers in a single night. . . . They've actually evolved differences in shape and physiology as well. Essentially, they have turned into these dispersal machines and they move as far as they can, as fast as they can."[15] And the toads have adapted to a variety of climates. They now live in bitterly cold regions, dry deserts, and wet tropical ecosystems.

## Blood-Drinking Invaders

Cane toads might pose major problems for native species, but they do not harm people. However, some invasive species spread deadly diseases that are alarming public health officials. The Asian tiger mosquito is one such invader. Named for the distinctive black and white tiger-like stripes on its body and legs, the Asian tiger mosquito ranks among the world's hundred worst invasive species, according to the Global Invasive Species Index.

The Asian tiger mosquito is native to the warm, humid tropical forests of Southeast Asia, where it is active year-round. Since the 1960s, the mosquito has spread through shipping and international travel to inhabit warm regions, including South and Central America, the Caribbean, Africa, and the Middle East. The mosquito also evolved to hibernate in the winter, which allowed it

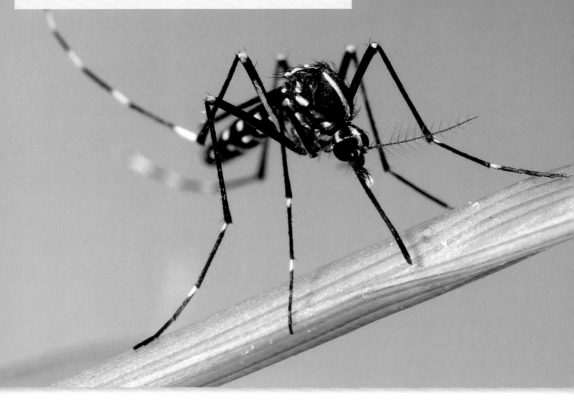

Asian tiger mosquitoes, like the one pictured here, are among the world's worst invasive species. These mosquitoes are carriers of deadly viral diseases such as dengue fever, yellow fever, Chikungunya fever, and the Zika virus.

to gain a foothold in the colder regions of Europe. The first Asian tiger mosquito in the United States was spotted in Texas in 1980, and it only took one year to spread nearly 800 miles (1,287 km) from Houston to St. Louis, Missouri. Asian tiger mosquito eggs, which evolved to tolerate snow and freezing temperatures, helped the blood-sucking insect invade wintery states like Illinois, Iowa, New Jersey, and Vermont.

Like other mosquito species, female Asian tiger mosquitoes require blood to develop eggs and reproduce. They drink the blood of birds and mammals, including humans. Females lay eggs near standing water in bowls, buckets, animal dishes, flower pots, and puddles. Used car and truck tires that hold rainwater have been instrumental in spreading the Asian tiger mosquito around the world.

All mosquitoes are pests, but the Asian tiger mosquito is particularly deadly. It is a carrier of viral diseases, including dengue (pronounced DENG-ay) fever, yellow fever, Chikungunya fever, and the Zika virus. These diseases cause rashes, severe headaches, muscle pain, fever, chills, nausea, vomiting, and death. The mosquitoes also transmit a parasite that causes heartworm in dogs and cats. Tiger mosquitoes spread avian malaria, which has been killing endangered species of forest birds in Hawaii.

Throughout history, tropical diseases like dengue fever, yellow fever, and the Zika virus were unknown in temperate climates. For example, in 1970 only nine countries experienced dengue fever outbreaks. During the thirty years since the worldwide invasion of the Asian tiger mosquito, the disease has been seen in more than one hundred countries, including the United States. And as the globe warms from climate change, researchers expect Asian tiger mosquitoes to move farther north to Minnesota, Wisconsin, Canada, Siberia, and other frigid regions.

The war against invading insects, amphibians, plants, and other species is only beginning, even as new invaders are being discovered every year. While scientists work to slow the damage, the task will remain difficult as people and the goods they produce continue to circle the globe in record numbers.

# Chapter Three

# Forests Fall, Diversity Shrinks

Around two thousand years ago, Mayan people began building stunning stone cities and ornate temples in the southern part of Central America. Over the centuries the Mayans developed advanced systems of writing, mathematics, astronomy, and agriculture. They built around forty cities, and their population grew to roughly 20 million. The Mayans relied on predictable seasonal rains that provided them with abundant crops. But the spread of Mayan civilization took a toll on the environment. Buildings and crops replaced the dense tropical forests that had been thriving in the region for millennia.

With the loss of native species, the climate in the region began to change. For centuries the rain forest absorbed the sun's energy. The plants released water vapor that rose into the sky and fell back to the earth as rain. But after the forest was cut down, it could no longer perform this function. During the tenth century, rainfall decreased by about half and temperatures rose. Biodiversity loss, drought, and food shortages triggered warfare and political breakdowns. Mayan civilization collapsed within a few decades.

## Slash-and-Burn Agriculture

The rise and fall of Mayan civilization had little effect on the Yanomami people who lived in the Amazon rain forest in South America. Today around thirty-five thousand Yanomami live in northern Brazil and southeastern Venezuela. Some have been exposed to Western culture and live in the modern world, but the majority of the Yanomami continue to follow the ways of their ancestors. They obtain all of their food, medicine, clothing, and housing from the rain forest. The forest provides the Yanomami with the leaves, vines, and tree trunks they use to build their communal houses, called *shabanos*. Yanomami men traditionally hunt a wide variety of native animals, including snakes, monkeys, deer, jaguars, and fish, but about 90 percent of the Yanomami diet is plant based.

Yanomami women forage in the forest for wild fruits and nuts, some of which are familiar to modern shoppers: passion fruit, papaya, açaí berries, Brazil nuts, and cacao (the key ingredient in chocolate). Yanomami women also tend small gardens planted with starchy tuber–producing shrubs called cassava, along with beans and sweet potatoes, which are native to the region. The Yanomami also cultivate corn, or maize, which was first domesticated in southern Mexico around ten thousand years ago.

**IMPACT FACTS**

The Amazon rain forest is roughly the size of the forty-eight contiguous United States, covering 2.7 million square miles (6.9 million km$^2$).

—Rhett A. Butler, environmental journalist

The Yanomami practice slash-and-burn agriculture. They create farm fields by cutting down trees and other plants. This creates what is called slash, which is left to dry. When the slash is burned, the soil is fertilized by the ash that is left behind. However, the soil nutrients provided by the ash are depleted within three to five years. Weeds and pests overtake the depleted area, and the Yanomami move on to new areas to begin the process again.

The desire to turn forests into farm fields is as old as humanity, and slash-and-burn farming is sustainable when practiced by a small group. However, the practice is not sustainable for large populations. Huge tracts of the Amazon rain forest are being slashed and burned on an industrial scale in Brazil, Peru, Bolivia, and elsewhere and not by indigenous peoples like the Yanomami.

Yanomami women carry their children through Venezuela's Amazon rain forest. The indigenous Yanomami still use the same slash-and-burn techniques practiced by the ancient Mayans to convert forests to farm fields.

Farmers and ranchers are turning ancient forests into pastures for beef cattle and soybean fields to grow feed for pigs, chickens, and other livestock.

One acre (0.4 ha) of rain forest might have 480 tree species, whereas a single bush in the Amazon may have more species of ants than the entire British Isles. When these forests are logged, burned, and converted to farmland, the result is large-scale loss of species. And as with the Yanomami fields, the tracts used by ranchers are only productive for three to five years. Then new areas need to be cleared. According to biology professor Brian Farrell, "The production of cattle and soybeans is one of the least-sustainable and less economically valuable uses of the rainforests."[16]

## Wildfires and Wildlife

Although deliberately burning the rain forest is illegal in the nine nations where the Amazon is located, the laws are rarely enforced. In 2019 the lack of environmental oversite in the Amazon made headlines around the world. In August, at least eighty thousand fires raged in Brazil alone, and smoke from the fires was visible from outer space. While two-thirds of the rain forest is in Brazil, fires also consumed forests in Paraguay, Bolivia, Peru, and other nations. In all, an estimated 3,500 square miles (9,060 km$^2$) of rain forest were deliberately set on fire, an increase of 80 percent over 2018.

The Amazon rain forest is often referred to as the lungs of the earth because the trees and plants remove climate-warming carbon dioxide and release oxygen into the atmosphere through the process of photosynthesis. Fires release huge quantities of that stored carbon.

Fire is a natural occurrence in northern forests, where species have adapted to the periodic wildfires. When fires burn an area, birds, mammals, and other creatures move somewhere else. But the damp Amazon rain forest evolved for millions of years without fire, and the native animals lack the natural ability to adapt to changing environmental circumstances. Some of the species threatened by fires in the Amazon include the rare Amazonian jaguar, giant otters, and several species of monkey, including the white-cheeked spider monkey and the golden lion tamarin. The tapir, a Yanomami food source, is also threatened. Farrell writes, "These widespread fires are driving wildlife away from their habitats and territories, with resulting catastrophic losses. The life and livelihoods of the Yanomami and other indigenous peoples are under threat not seen since the first Europeans entered South America [during the early 1500s]."[17]

## IMPACT FACTS

In 2019 around 3,500 square miles (9,060 km$^2$) of rain forest were burned for agricultural purposes, an increase of 80 percent over 2018.

—National Institute for Space Research, Brazil

## The Demand for Meat

Around 20 percent of the Amazon has already been deforested, and an equal area has been negatively impacted by activities such

## Reaching a Tipping Point

The loss of biodiversity has been blamed for the collapse of ancient Mayan society and numerous other bygone cultures. Environmental degradation helped trigger the downfall of Sumer, the world's earliest civilization in what is now Iraq. Minoan society on the isle of Crete, Viking settlements in Greenland, and the Tang dynasty of China were all devastated by environmental catastrophes. Although these problems were confined to relatively small areas, widespread fires in today's Amazon rain forest might have devastating global consequences. As biology professor Brian Farrell explains,

> The great fear is that the loss of habitat [in the Amazon] will cross a threshold of no return, a tipping point for transformation of climate cycles that will result in new rainfall patterns. The rainfall cycles in the Amazon depend on transfer of water through rainforest plants to the atmosphere, where it eventually condenses as rain that is delivered over a very broad region, again sustaining rainforest plants as well as much of the continent. If fire removes the plant life responsible for moving water up into the clouds, the land will dry and rainforests will be replaced by grasslands able to withstand the newly arid conditions, which can persist for thousands of years. This has occurred in the Americas and elsewhere in prehistoric times. The economic and ecological consequences for the cities that today depend on these sources of atmospheric water, as well as the natural ecosystems and indigenous peoples they support, will be devastating.

Quoted in Colleen Walsh, "Amazon Blazes Could Speed Climate Change," *Harvard Gazette,* August 28, 2019. http://news.harvard.edu.

as road construction, mining, and other activities. And the loss of forest biodiversity extends far beyond the Amazon. According to a study by the Wildlife Conservation Society, human activity is threatening 80 percent of the world's forests with destruction. This is putting about half of the world's biodiversity at risk.

One reason rain forests are falling is that the worldwide demand for meat has quadrupled since 1970. While meat is an important source of nutrition for millions of people, livestock production has major environmental costs. Excrement from cows, pigs, chickens, and other livestock pollutes rivers and wetlands, destroying biodiversity while sickening local populations that depend on freshwater for drinking and washing. And according to the United Nations, animal agriculture is responsible for 18 percent of all global greenhouse gas emissions.

Brazil is the world's largest beef exporter; the nation provided around 20 percent of total global beef exports in 2019 and is projected to produce 23 percent by 2028. Although China and Hong Kong import the most Brazilian beef, nearly 141 million pounds (64 million kg) were shipped to the United States in 2019. This was a relatively small portion of the record-setting 27.4 billion pounds (12.4 billion kg) of beef consumed by Americans that year.

## IMPACT FACTS

Americans consumed a record 27.4 billion pounds (12.4 billion kg) of beef in 2019.

—Derrell Peel, agricultural economist

## Palm Oil Plantations

While cattle ranching is responsible for rain forest destruction in South America, the growing demand for palm oil has fueled biodiversity crises in Malaysia, Indonesia, and elsewhere in the tropics. Palm oil, which has been used for cooking for thousands of years, comes from the fruit of the African oil palm. This extremely versatile vegetable oil, which is cheap to produce, is used today in thousands of consumer products. Palm oil acts as a foaming agent in 70 percent of personal care products, including soaps and shampoos, and is used to add creaminess to lipstick and other cosmetics. The oil can be found in detergents, polishes, candles, and livestock feed.

Palm oil is used as an additive in around half of the packaged foods on supermarket shelves, including potato chips, cookies, chocolate, bread, milk, and ice cream. Fast food restaurants such as Domino's Pizza, Subway, KFC, McDonald's and Dunkin'

Donuts are major consumers of palm oil. In Europe, palm oil is used as a clean-burning biofuel to power cars and trucks in place of polluting diesel fuel.

The versatility of palm oil has created a massive worldwide demand. Production of palm oil quadrupled between 1995 and 2015 and is expected to quadruple again by 2050. In 2019 around half of the people on Earth used products that contained palm oil, each person consuming an average of 18 pounds (8 kg) annually. But the growing use of palm oil has come with a steep environmental cost.

Around 87 percent of all palm oil is produced in two countries—Malaysia and Indonesia—where large areas of tropical forests have been cleared for palm oil plantations. Indonesia is being deforested faster than any other nation on Earth. As with the Amazon, the fast-

Workers harvest palm fruit on a palm oil plantation in Indonesia. Around 87 percent of all palm oil is produced in Malaysia and Indonesia, where large areas of tropical forests have been cleared for palm oil plantations.

est and cheapest way to clear the land is though slash-and-burn operations. The forests being destroyed for palm oil plantations are the most carbon rich in the world; the fires are the top source of greenhouse gas emissions in Indonesia, a nation of more than 260 million people.

## Orangutans, Tigers, and Elephants

According to the International Union for Conservation of Nature, 193 endangered and vulnerable species are threatened by palm oil production in South America, Africa, Asia, and elsewhere. And the organization says that if palm oil production continues to grow as predicted, it could affect 54 percent of all threatened mammals and 64 percent of all threatened birds globally. The problem of palm oil and biodiversity loss is exemplified by the situation on the Indonesian island of Sumatra and the neighboring island of Borneo, part of which is governed by Indonesia and part by Malaysia. These two islands provide critical habitat for endangered species, including Sumatran tigers, Sumatran rhinos, Sumatran elephants, Sunda clouded leopards, Bornean pygmy elephants, crested black macaque monkeys, small apes known as gibbons, and sun bears.

Palm oil production is also the leading threat to orangutans. As palm oil plantations expanded on Borneo between 1999 and 2015, the number of orangutans declined by one hundred thousand. In Sumatra, where half the island's trees have been cut down since 1985, there are only fourteen thousand orangutans left in the wild. Whereas some orangutans are killed by fires set to clear the land, others are marooned in small areas of rain forest surrounded by palm oil plantations. When desperately hungry orangutans wander onto the plantations in search of food, they are routinely shot.

Some palm oil is grown in a sustainable manner in places where critical habitat is not endangered. But palm oil is so widely used that it will take a global effort to slow the deforestation and resulting biodiversity loss that is caused by the unsustainable production of this product.

## Bird Loss in the United States

Many Americans criticize nations like Malaysia and Brazil for cutting down old-growth forests, but much of the United States has been deforested since European settlers first arrived during the mid-1600s. Forests once covered nearly 1 billion acres (404.7 million ha), or one-third of the land. By the end of the nineteenth century, around 90 percent of the old-growth forests that had once covered the United States had been chopped down. Much of the cleared land was given over to crops and livestock pastures. During the twentieth century, many of those fields were paved over for suburbs and highways. The forests that exist today are known as second-growth (although they might be third- or even fourth-growth forests). These woodlands, which grew back after the old-growth trees were logged, lack the biodiversity of the original forests.

The continuing loss of forest habitat in the United States is responsible for a biodiversity crisis that is threatening bees, but-

## Medicine from the Forest

Scientists have only studied around 10 percent of the eighty thousand plant species found in the Amazon rain forest. But research shows that the Amazon is a rich source for natural medicinal compounds. Around 25 percent of all drugs used today in modern medicine are derived from rain forest plants. And researchers are hoping the next generation of miracle drugs will come from the Amazon.

The US National Cancer Institute says that 70 percent of plants with potential anticancer properties grow only in the Amazon rain forest. Some of these species include a woody vine called cat's claw, employed by the indigenous Yanomami to treat rheumatism and toothaches, and the sap of the sangre de grado tree, which is used to stop bleeding. A wood shrub called amargo produces a bitter compound traditionally used to treat fever and malaria. This plant contains chemicals that researchers hope to use one day to treat diabetes, ulcers, and leukemia. An herbal preparation called lapacho, made from the pau d'arco tree, contains properties that are antifungal, antimicrobial, antiviral, and anti-inflammatory.

terflies, frogs, and dozens of other animals and plants. Nowhere has this loss been more profound than among the hundreds of once-common bird species in North America.

Forests would not exist without the billions of birds that play an essential role in sustaining biodiversity. Birds pollinate flowers, control insects and other pests, and regenerate forests by spreading seeds. Most bird species traditionally reproduce in large numbers—and they are the best-monitored animals in North America. Thousands of bird watchers have been participating in two annual counts for decades: the North American Breeding Bird Survey and the Christmas Bird Count. These studies provide valuable data that allows researchers to keep a tally of numerous species.

According to an extensive analysis of 529 species by the journal *Science,* America's bird populations are in steep decline. The number of forest birds, including the wood thrush and the Baltimore oriole, have dropped by 22 percent since 1970. The crisis is worse among grassland birds, whose numbers have declined by

53 percent since 1970, and shorebirds, which have experienced a 37 percent loss since 1974. These numbers translate to a loss of nearly 3 billion birds in fifty years. And the losses are affecting the most common bird species, such as sparrows, swallows, warblers, and finches, along with rarer species, such as whooping cranes and woodpeckers. Conservation scientist Kenneth V. Rosenberg commented on the study: "We were stunned by the result—it's just staggering. . . . It's not just these highly threatened birds that we're afraid are going to go on the endangered species list. It's across the board."[18]

## Forests Mean Survival

What happened in the United States in the past is happening today in tropical rain forests. But the consequences of this modern deforestation might be catastrophic. As indigenous leader Davi Kopenawa Yanomami says,

> People think that the forest was laid on the ground for no purpose, as if it was lifeless. This is not true. . . . If the forest was dead, the trees would not have shiny leaves. Nor would there be water on earth. Our forest is alive, and if white people make us disappear in order to cut it down and live in our place, they will be poor and will end up suffering from hunger and thirst.[19]

While modern city dwellers might think that they are not dependent on rain forest biodiversity for their survival, Yanomami's words serve as a warning to all. Trees and plants scrub carbon dioxide from the atmosphere, and the forests provide sustenance to countless species that can live nowhere else. Not only do these species need to be protected for their own sake, but the survival of *Homo sapiens* is dependent on them. As the ancient Mayans learned, the natural world can help civilizations rise, but societies can rapidly fall when the natural balance of the forest meets the ax and the torch.

# Chapter Four

# Threats to Ocean Ecosystems

Gene Feldman is an oceanographer who has studied the world's oceans for more than thirty-five years. Feldman says this planet might be called Earth, but it really should be called Ocean. "Life on land . . . begins a few feet below the surface of the soil and extends up into the tops of the trees," Feldman asserts. "But in the ocean, life is found all the way from the surface to the . . . deepest part of the ocean [which] is nearly seven-and-a-half miles (12 km) down. Because of this, the oceans contain 99 percent of the living space on the planet."[20]

With all that living space, the oceans nourish more biodiversity than any ecosystems on land. But Feldman also notes that scientists know more about the surface of Mars and the Moon than they do about the ocean; it is easier to launch a rocket to Mars than to explore the pitch-black, frigid ocean depths where the pressure can be over one thousand times higher than on land. In this inhospitable environment, scientists have only been able to identify a tiny number of species of the deep sea and polar oceans. This makes the loss of ocean species harder to record and analyze. But oceanographers and marine biologists who study ocean ecosystems closer to the surface have seen a dramatic decrease in biological diversity since the mid-twentieth century. The oceans are threatened by overfishing, pollution, and climate change.

## Acidic Oceans

The oceans support all life on Earth through a web of biodiversity that begins with microscopic plants called phytoplankton. These tiny plants have evolved into a large number of species that provide the basis for the aquatic food chain that sustains all life in the ocean. Tiny shrimp-like creatures called krill feed on phytoplankton. The krill found in the icy waters of Antarctica are the most abundant species on the planet in terms of biomass, or total weight.

The ocean food chain can be imagined as a giant pyramid with phytoplankton and krill making up the massive foundation. The next level is inhabited by small fish that eat krill, larger fish that feed on smaller ones, and top ocean predators like orcas, great white sharks, and barracudas that consume larger fish. The next level of the pyramid would be occupied by fish-eating marine creatures like penguins, seals, and walruses. Humans also occupy this level: 3 billion people depend on seafood for survival. If the bottom layer of the phytoplankton/krill food pyramid is reduced, the layers above can collapse. The entire food chain loses its ability to support life at the top.

# IMPACT FACTS

Burning fossil fuels has made the oceans more acidic than they have been in the past 14 million years.

—Sindia Sosdian, marine biochemist

While phytoplankton and krill are critical to life on Earth, these important species are threatened by fossil fuels used on land. When coal, oil, and natural gas are burned, carbon dioxide ($CO_2$) is released into the atmosphere. The oceans have absorbed around 30 percent of all $CO_2$ emitted by humans. When this $CO_2$ dissolves in seawater, a substance called carbonic acid is produced. This chemical reaction is causing oceans to become more acidic.

Ocean acidification is threatening sea creatures that build their shells or skeletons from calcium carbonate. These marine species, known as calcifying organisms, include coral, phytoplankton, krill, and marine invertebrates such as clams, oysters, crabs,

*The krill found in the icy waters of Antarctica (pictured) feed on microscopic phytoplankton and are the most abundant species on the planet in terms of biomass, or total weight.*

and sea snails. In addition to dissolving calcium, acid reduces the amount of calcium in seawater, making it more difficult for calcifying organisms to grow and thrive.

## Warming Seas

Ocean acidification is damaging coral reefs—colonies of living coral that are held together by calcium carbonate. Coral reefs grow in shallow, clear water where sunlight is abundant. They are sometimes referred to as rain forests of the sea because of their incredible biodiversity. While coral reefs occupy less than 0.1 percent of the total area of the ocean, they provide habitat to around 25 percent of all marine species. In 2011 scientists studying a 70-square-foot (6.5-m²) section of coral reef in India found 525 species of crustaceans, more than are found in the entire ocean system surrounding Europe. Large numbers of fish species, sponges, mollusks, sea worms, starfish, and sea urchins depend on coral reefs for survival.

The increase in ocean acidity is dissolving calcium carbonate coral skeletons. Coral reefs are also threatened by warming ocean temperatures that cause coral to bleach, or turn white. Healthy coral reefs are extremely colorful; they produce a startling array of hues ranging from fiery orange and deep purple to glowing pinks, reds, and greens. These colors are produced by multiple species of algae called *zooxanthellae* that have a symbiotic relationship with the coral.

Coral provides a protective environment for the algae, shielding them from fish and other predators. Coral also produces enzymes the algae need for photosynthesis. During the photosynthesis process the algae return the favor, releasing oxygen and chemicals such as glucose, which the coral need to produce calcium. However, climate change is interrupting this process. If seawater warms as little as 2°F (1°C), the coral expel the colorful algae, revealing the underlying white skeleton. Without the algae, the coral slowly starve. Coral can recover if it does not die before ocean temperatures return to normal levels.

Ocean temperatures vary from place to place and are affected by the seasons and the depth of the water. But climate change is causing phenomena called marine heat waves. The world's oceans are warming more frequently and for longer periods of time. According to a study by the journal *Nature,* between 1982 and 2016 the number of days with unusually high temperatures in upper ocean levels increased by 82 percent. This caused more than sixty major coral bleaching events around the world.

The largest coral reef is the Great Barrier Reef. This complex of around twenty-nine hundred reefs, an area bigger than Italy, stretches along the coast of Queensland, Australia. The Great Barrier Reef has been severely impacted by marine heat waves, experiencing five major bleaching events during the late twentieth century and four since 2002. In 2016 record-high temperatures in the Pacific Ocean killed one-third of the coral that makes up the Great Barrier Reef. Researchers were stunned when they found the once-vibrant, colorful reef had turned to a ghastly, skeletal white. Scientist Jodie Rummer stated, "I witnessed a sight underwater that no marine biologist, and no person with a love and appreciation for the natural world for that matter, wants to see."[21]

Coral reefs provide vitally important spawning and feeding grounds for countless species of marine life. Fish species like grouper and snapper use the maze of pathways between coral branches to hide from predators. Without the reefs, populations of these fish species would shrink, as would those of clams, oysters, lobsters, crabs, and other creatures.

Fish and other marine creatures sustained by coral provide food for half a billion people around the world. Without coral reefs,

## Carbon Dioxide and Seawater

Ocean acidification is discussed in terms of the pH value of the water; *pH* stands for "potential of hydrogen." It represents the number of hydrogen atoms in a substance on a numeric scale of 1 to 14 that specifies whether a liquid is acidic, neutral, or alkaline. Liquids with low pH values, around 1 or 2, are highly acidic; vinegar has a pH of 2.4. Distilled water is neutral with a pH of 7. A high pH value of 12 or 13 indicates a solution is highly alkaline. Coral and the shells of oysters, mussels, and other mollusks are made from calcium carbonate, a relatively alkaline substance with a pH of 9.9.

For millions of years the oceans maintained a pH of 8.2. But since the start of the Industrial Revolution about 250 years ago, the oceans have been absorbing the higher levels of atmospheric carbon dioxide, which when dissolved in water creates carbonic acid, which has a pH of 5.6. This has reduced the pH of the ocean to 8.1. Although a reduction from 8.2 to 8.1 pH might not sound like much, it is enough to create stress or even kill some organisms. Today the ocean is approximately 30 percent more acidic than it was during the eighteenth century—and seawater has not been this acidic in 14 million years. While the ocean is scrubbing $CO_2$ from the atmosphere, the acidification is impairing the growth rate and survival of critical ocean species, including phytoplankton, krill, coral, and mollusks.

Bleached coral is visible on the Great Barrier Reef off the coast of Queensland, Australia. In 2016 record-high temperatures in the Pacific Ocean killed one-third of the coral that makes up the Great Barrier Reef.

a major portion of the global ocean fishing industry would collapse, leaving around 38 million people unemployed. Environmental professor Sylvia Dee explains, "Corals are the foundation of ecosystem health for most marine species. If the corals go away, you lose the fish, you lose everything."[22]

## Kelp Forests

Whereas coral reefs provide biodiversity in tropical regions, kelp forests provide the same ecological benefits in cold ocean waters. Kelp is a type of algae, sometimes referred to as seaweed, that grows in the clear, nutrient-rich waters along the coasts of continents. Dense forests of kelp have been growing along one-quarter of all coastlines on Earth for at least 5 million years. Some of the largest and most biodiverse kelp forests in the world can be found along the Pacific Coast of North America. These ocean forests grow along the coasts of Alaska, down through Canada to California, and along the Baja California Peninsula in northwestern Mexico.

Kelp grows wherever sunlight can reach the ocean floor, and the algae has unique characteristics that allow it to thrive in the sea. Kelp does not have tree-like roots that dig into sand or soil. The algae anchor to the ocean floor with a root-like mass called a holdfast, which grips rocks and other objects. Kelp can grow incredibly fast, as much as 2 feet (0.6 m) a day, and some species attain a length of more than 175 feet (53 m). The algae are able to stay afloat with air-filled bladders called pneumatocysts, which grow on the stalks.

When various species of kelp grow together in a region, they create habitat on different levels, much like a forest on land. This can be observed in the kelp forests of the Channel Islands off the central coast of California. These forests are primarily made up of elk kelp, bull kelp, and giant kelp. Elk kelp, with its antler-like branches, grows in the deepest waters, where no other kelp will grow. Bull kelp, which reaches a length of 118 feet (36 m), makes up the middle layer of the kelp forest. Giant kelp occupies the top level and can stretch hundreds of feet from the sea bottom to the surface of the water.

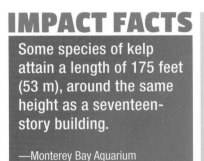

**IMPACT FACTS**

Some species of kelp attain a length of 175 feet (53 m), around the same height as a seventeen-story building.

—Monterey Bay Aquarium

From the lowest levels to the dense leaves on the surface, kelp forests create rich feeding grounds and nurseries for marine creatures. Holdfasts provide food for prawns, snails, bristle worms, tiny crustaceans called amphipods, and brittle stars, which are closely related to starfish. These creatures attract predators such as crabs, lobsters, jellyfish, and sea urchins. A wide range of fish species live in kelp forests, including rockfish, which are valuable to the commercial fishing industry. Ocean mammals such as seals, sea lions, and otters feed on fish, sea urchins, and other creatures that live in kelp forests. Marine mammals also seek shelter in kelp forests during storms. Gray whales can be found feeding in kelp forests, and they also use the forests to hide from predators like killer whales (orcas).

The rich biodiversity found in kelp forests provides sustenance for seabirds, including gulls, great blue herons, terns, cormorants, and egrets. When kelp breaks off and washes ashore, the slimy leaves and stems attract sand flies, maggots, and worms, which feed crows, starlings, warblers, and other land birds.

## An Urchin Invasion

Kelp forests are food-generating ecosystems that have been supporting human populations for hundreds of thousands of years. They provide breeding grounds for fish, shellfish, and other seafood, and dried seaweed is an important addition to Chinese, Korean, and Japanese cuisine. A thick gum called alginate, which is derived from kelp, is used to thicken ice cream, salad dressings, and toothpaste. But when one piece of the food web is removed, the entire kelp forest ecosystem is impacted. And nothing exemplifies the fragility of kelp forest biodiversity better than the purple urchin invasion in Northern California and Oregon.

Kelp forests have been struggling as the Pacific Ocean warms from climate change. Giant kelp grows best in waters where average temperatures are 50°F to 60°F (10°C to 16°C). But between 2014 and 2016, a large mass of warm water raised ocean temperatures along the West Coast around 9°F (5°C) above average. Researchers called this massive area of warm water "the Blob" because it appeared as a giant red blob on ocean surface temperature maps. The Blob returned in September 2019. This time it was given a technical name—the Northeast Pacific Marine Heatwave of 2019.

Scientists believe the first appearance of the Blob in 2014 caused a disease called sea star wasting syndrome, which wiped out millions of starfish. The hardest-hit species, the sunflower sea

## Seafood Problems

Nearly half of the people on Earth depend on fish and other types of seafood as their main source of protein. Around half of this seafood is farm raised in tanks and other enclosures. But the seafood industry that harvests fish from the wild has had a significant impact on biodiversity. According to the Food and Agriculture Organization of the United Nations, 85 percent of marine fisheries (fishing grounds) are either fully exploited or overfished. Those that are fully exploited can yield no more fish. Those that are overfished are having fish removed at unsustainable levels and are at risk of collapsing. In 2019, more than fourteen hundred species of fish—or 5 percent of the world's known species—were at risk of extinction. Some of these are well-known commercial species, including orange roughy, Atlantic cod, and bluefin tuna.

Fishing crews do more than pull commercially valuable fish from the ocean; some of the most popular fishing practices are destructive to ocean habitat. A technique called seafloor trawling, or bottom trawling, involves dragging large nets across the ocean floor. On the West Coast these nets, which can weigh several tons, are used to catch rockfish, halibut, and sole. As the nets are pulled along, they destroy large swaths of ocean floor habitat; as much as 90 percent of coral colonies and up to two-thirds of sponges are destroyed by bottom trawlers. The nets also ensnare and kill millions of creatures with no commercial value, including turtles and dolphins. Although fish can be sustainably harvested from the oceans, the fishing industry is largely unregulated in many parts of the world.

star, is one of the most colorful starfish in the ocean. While pleasing to the eye, the sunflower sea star plays an important role in the kelp forest ecosystem. The sea star is the only predator of the purple sea urchin, which feeds on kelp. The disappearance of the sea stars created a sea urchin population boom. In 2019, around 350 million purple sea urchins were counted along a single reef in Oregon, a 10,000 percent increase since 2014.

The spiny purple urchins are creating what are called urchin barrens—vast areas of denuded seafloor where kelp forests once thrived. In Northern California 90 percent of the kelp forests have

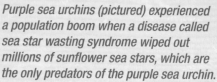

Purple sea urchins (pictured) experienced a population boom when a disease called sea star wasting syndrome wiped out millions of sunflower sea stars, which are the only predators of the purple sea urchin.

been replaced by urchin barrens. In addition to threatening biodiversity, the urchin invasion is having an impact on fisheries. Red abalone and red sea urchins, which are harvested for sushi, have disappeared.

In some places, purple urchins have nearly eaten themselves into starvation by consuming all the kelp. But when this happens, the urchins can stop reproducing and lay dormant for years. Although purple urchins can be eaten, the edible part shrivels when they are dormant, making them worthless.

Parts of the Oregon coast used to be so dense with kelp that boats could not navigate the waters. Now there is just blue, open water. And scientists fear that kelp forests—and sea stars—might never return. Ecology professor Mark Carr commented on the situation: "We know we're going to see more warming in the future because of global climate change so who knows if we will see more of these purple urchin outbreaks. You do wonder whether we're transitioning into a new environmental dynamic that we just haven't seen in the past."[23]

## Explore the Oceans

While much of the vast ocean is unexplored, the sudden decline of kelp forests and coral reefs close to shore demonstrates the fragility of marine ecosystems that have existed for eons. Plastic pollution and toxic chemicals pose more threats to ocean biodiversity, and the consequences of this contamination remain unknown. Likewise, overfishing is threatening many species, including Atlantic halibut, monkfish, bluefin tuna, and sharks.

All life on Earth came from the sea, and the well-being of humanity—and thousands of other species—depends on the health of the oceans. The way forward lies in learning more about the oceans. Some scientists believe it is time to create a well-funded ocean exploration program that rivals the space program in terms of money and pioneering research. As oceanographer Feldman says, "There are things about this wonderful planet that are still a mystery. There are questions that can keep scientists busy for as long as there are people on this planet. . . . Science is . . . the only way that we can take care of this amazing place we call home."[24]

# Chapter Five

# Addressing Problems, Reducing Threats

In 2019, sixteen-year-old Swedish environmental activist Greta Thunberg was named Person of the Year by *Time* magazine. Thunberg first gained media attention when she initiated a one-person environmental protest in August 2018. Thunberg skipped out of her ninth-grade classes to sit outside the Swedish Parliament holding a homemade sign that read "School Strike for Climate"[25] When a reporter asked her what she was doing, Thunberg said she was planning to cut school every Friday until Sweden passed laws that drastically reduced carbon emissions.

An article about Thunberg appeared in a local paper, and within a week her simple message had launched a movement called Fridays for Future. Swedish students, teachers, parents, and activists joined the climate strike, which attracted widespread media attention. Within a month the campaign had gone viral on social media. By November 2018, seventeen thousand students in twenty-four countries were participating in Fridays for Future climate strikes. Thunberg became an international sensation as her simple message galvanized the world. In March 2019 Thunberg was nominated for a Nobel Peace Prize.

In September 2019 an estimated 6 million people of all ages and backgrounds joined in international climate strikes known as the Global Week for Future. In what has been called the biggest climate protest ever held, people took to the streets in more than six hundred cities in the United States, Europe, Africa, and the Middle East. As climate week unfolded, Thunberg gave a speech at the United Nations that was blunt and to the point: "We are in the beginning of a mass extinction, and all you can talk about is money and fairy tales of eternal economic growth. How dare you."[26]

*Sixteen-year-old Swedish environmental activist Greta Thunberg (pictured) speaks at a press conference in New York City in 2019. Thunberg was named Time magazine's 2019 Person of the Year.*

## Shifting Paradigms

The fact that Thunberg's protest rapidly blasted into a world-wide movement shows that people are hungry to address climate change, biodiversity loss, and other environmental problems. Even before Thunberg began making headlines, other students were hard at work drawing attention to the climate crisis. In 2017 a sixteen-year-old Seattle student named Jamie Margolin started an environmental group called Zero Hour. The group organizes marches and works to get pro-environment politicians elected to office.

Margolin appeared before the US Congress in 2019. She gave testimony in support of the Green New Deal, a resolution introduced by Representative Alexandria Ocasio-Cortez. The Green New Deal proposes that United States move to 100 percent renewable energy by 2029. The ambitious plan promises to phase out gasoline-powered vehicles and overhaul transportation, housing, agriculture, forestry, and other systems in order to slow climate change and reduce biodiversity loss. Although the political fate of the Green New Deal remained hazy, Margolin has expressed optimism. "The good news is that experts agree there are multiple pathways to decarbonize the U.S. energy system and that doing so is technologically and economically viable,"[27] she said.

Some of the experts working to decarbonize energy systems are scientists. While many avoided advocacy in the past—content to let their research do the talking—some are now voicing their concerns. In 2019 around fifteen hundred scientists from around the world signed a petition to signal their support for a London-based environmental group called Extinction Rebellion. The group organized mass sit-in demonstrations that closed down major streets and disrupted traffic in sixty cities for ten days. Extinction Rebellion demands that politicians declare a climate emergency and take steps to address biodiversity loss, ocean acidification, and deforestation. Atmospheric chemist Scott Archer-Nicholls

Supporters of the Extinction Rebellion climate change movement gather in London in 2018. The group demands that politicians declare a climate emergency and take steps to address biodiversity loss, ocean acidification, and deforestation.

joined the group's demonstration in front of Parliament in London. He recalled, "The rate these [environmental] movements grew took me by surprise, I did not think I would see their like until it was too late. . . . People seemed genuinely worried about climate change and were involved for good moral reasons."[28]

When enough people demand government action, their voices can create a paradigm shift—a completely new way of doing things. The paradigm has shifted before on the environment. Up until the late 1960s, oil and chemical companies, steel mills, power plants, and other industrial polluters fouled the air and water with few consequences. People protested, the Earth Day movement was founded in 1970, and the industrial system was rapidly transformed. Politicians followed the will of the people and enacted new laws that drastically changed the way business was done. Thanks to this paradigm shift, the skies and waterways today are remarkably cleaner than they were during the 1960s.

Jamie Margolin was sixteen when she founded the environmental group Zero Hour in Seattle in 2017. In 2019 Margolin appeared before the US Congress in support of the Green New Deal, a resolution aimed at addressing biodiversity loss and the climate crisis. What follows is an excerpt of her testimony:

> The shellfish, salmon, orcas, and all of the beautiful wildlife of my Pacific Northwest home is dying due to ocean acidification caused by the climate crisis. . . . Is this the future we have to look forward to? We the youth are working to make sure it isn't. . . . This past July of 2019, Zero Hour organized the Youth Climate Summit, in Miami Florida, where we educated and united roughly 350 young people from across the country on climate action. Throughout the entirety of 2019 we have implemented a campaign called Getting To The Roots of Climate Change, where we have trained over 600 youth climate justice ambassadors (and counting) to educate their communities. . . . We are bringing a delegation of youth to the upcoming UN climate summit, where our voices will be heard by leaders from around the world. . . . By 2030, I will be old enough to run for congress and be seated where you are right now. By then we need to have already achieved net zero greenhouse gas emissions and be rapidly on the path to climate recovery.

Jamie Margolin, "Jamie Margolin's 2019 Congressional Testimony," House of Representatives, September 18, 2019. https://docs.house.gov/meetings/FA/FA14/20190918/109951/HHRG-116-FA14-Wstate -MargolinJ-20190918.pdf.

## Building a Better Burger

Today another paradigm shift is under way. People are thinking differently about the food they consume and are changing the way they eat in order to reduce biodiversity loss and preserve forests. According to the Johns Hopkins Center for a Livable Future, between 30 and 50 percent of Americans are interested in cutting down on the amount of meat they eat. Some are driven by health concerns; medical studies continue to link consumption of processed meat and red meat to chronic diseases. But an increasing number of people are changing their diet based on environmental concerns; the clearing of land to feed and raise livestock has led to an unprecedented extinction crisis.

Getting people to give up their burgers and steaks to slow down deforestation is the main goal of some of the richest people on Earth. Amazon.com founder Jeff Bezos, Microsoft founder Bill Gates, Virgin Group founder Richard Branson, and other billionaires have invested nearly $400 million in a company called Impossible Foods, which produces the meatless Impossible Burger. Unlike most vegetarian burgers, the Impossible Burger tastes surprisingly beef-like and even "bleeds" like a typical hamburger. The secret ingredient is an oxygen-carrying molecule called heme, which is found in plants, animals, and other living organisms. In animals, heme gives blood its red color.

Biochemist Patrick O. Brown founded Impossible Foods in 2011 after he discovered a way to use a genetically modified heme molecule to create vegan burgers that look and taste like beef burgers. Brown raised millions of dollars from investors and launched the Impossible Burg-er in 2016. By 2019, Impossible Foods was churning out millions of pounds of the plant-based burger per month. The meat-substitute patties were available in more than ten thousand locations throughout the United States, including White Castle, Carl's Jr., and other popu-lar fast food restaurants. After Burger King put the Impossible Whopper on its menu, the company saw a 6 percent increase in total sales.

**IMPACT FACTS**

Around 2 billion people worldwide live primarily on a meat-based diet.

—David Pimentel, professor of evolutionary biology

According to the Impossible Foods website, the vegan burg-ers are produced using 95 percent less land and 74 percent less water than hamburgers. The Impossible Burger also produces 87 percent fewer greenhouse gas emissions when compared to beef burgers. Impossible Foods is now working to produce heme-based steaks and pork sausage.

## Eating Burgers and Saving Species

In 2019 Kierán Suckling, founding member of the Center for Biological Diversity, released a statement in support of plant-based burgers from the companies Impossible Foods and Beyond Meat:

> Meat production is driving the extinction crisis by promoting the slaughter of wolves, bears, beavers and lions. It's polluting communities and waterways with toxic manure and poisoning the land with deadly pesticides used for growing feed. It's driving our climate emergency by bulldozing forests and belching out dangerous methane. Impossible Foods and Beyond Meat are doing us all an important service by pushing meat alternatives into mainstream culture at a level we haven't seen before. By speeding up the transition we desperately need to make toward plant-based eating, they're helping to save people, wildlife and our endangered planet.
>
> While other plant-based burgers have long been available, they have not dramatically altered the dietary choices of meat eaters, who make up the majority of the U.S. population. The mainstreaming of Beyond and Impossible burgers is changing this: About 90% of customers ordering Impossible Whoppers at Burger King are meat eaters, and 86% of people who eat plant-based meat alternatives are not vegan or vegetarian. Every plant-based burger they consume instead of beef reduces the demand for meat. More than 1 in 3 Americans eats fast food each day. To change our food system, we have to meet people where they are, including at the drive-thru. The existence of widely available meat alternatives that appeal to, and are being embraced by, meat eaters is an important step for a living planet.

Kierán Suckling, "Center for Biological Diversity Endorses Impossible, Beyond Burgers," Center for Biological Diversity, December 11, 2019. https://biologicaldiversity.org.

Some vegetarians have criticized Impossible Foods for using genetically modified ingredients, which they believe are unsafe for human consumption. But according to Brown, "The fact that heme is produced by genetic engineering is a complete non-issue from a consumer safety standpoint. It's a way safer way to produce [burgers] . . . than covering the entire frigging planet with cows, which is the way we're doing it now."[29]

Brown did not create the Impossible Burger for people who shun meat. The goal of Impossible Foods is to reduce deforestation and slow climate change by convincing millions of average consumers to eat less meat, though many are reluctant to do so. In 2019 the Center for Biological Diversity supported Brown's goal, endorsing Impossible Burgers and another brand of plant-based meat substitute called Beyond Burgers. The center's director, Kierán Suckling, maintains, "It's estimated that by 2040, 60% of meat will be plant-based or from other alternatives to animal agriculture. This rapid increase will . . . transform food systems . . . eliminating the worst pesticides from supply chains, embracing sustainable agriculture, and promoting pollinator-friendly agricultural practices."[30]

## Reforesting with Drones

Whereas some people are changing their diets, others are looking for innovative tech solutions to undo the damage caused by habitat loss, overexploitation of resources, and climate change. A British company called Dendra Systems (formerly called Bio-Carbon Engineering) thinks it has a solution to deforestation that addresses all three of these problems. In 2013 a NASA engineer suggested to environmental activist Irina Fedorenko that drones could be used to plant tree seeds. The next year, Fedorenko joined forces with biomedical engineer Susan Graham to found Dendra Systems, a company that designs and builds reforestation drones.

Forests currently remove about 25 percent of human-made $CO_2$ from the atmosphere, and one of the chief means to counter climate change involves reforestation. According to *National Geographic,* around 502,000 square miles (1.3 million km²) of forest have been cut down or burned in wildfires since 1990. But planting trees by hand is slow and costly. Dendra tackled the problem by engineering quadcopter drones (with four propellers), which are about 3 feet (1 m) wide, that can take over the backbreaking work of planting trees. The drones make high-resolution maps of an area. The data is fed into computers that analyze soil type, moisture levels, and topography (the shape and features of the land surface). This complex information is used by six drones flying in a swarm 6 feet (2 m) above the area. The drones fire what Dendra calls seed missiles into the ground, using compressed air technology borrowed from paint guns. Each seed missile contains a marble-sized pod holding a tree seed. The seed pod can also be packed with various types of bacteria and fungi that restore degraded soils and even neutralize toxic waste.

Working at full speed, the drones can plant four hundred thousand trees a day. It would take an army of human tree planters to match this number, and they would not have the data on soil and topography to help them plant the trees in optimum growing conditions. After trees are planted, the drones return to the site to monitor the growth of the new trees, down to individual seedlings. And Dendra plants a biodiverse range of trees that help restore the soil and create new habitat for endangered species. Fedorenko claims, "With our technology we can plant 150 times faster and ten times cheaper than the current planting methods used. . . . The present methods will take at least 200 years to restore the degraded land, and we don't have that time to fight climate change."[31]

## Harnessing Artificial Intelligence

Dendra's tree-planting drones rely on artificial intelligence (AI) software to analyze data such as annual rainfall, topography, and seasonal temperature changes. This information is used to program drones to plant seeds in ultraefficient patterns. The power of artificial intelligence is being harnessed elsewhere by scientists working on environmental sustainability.

Artificial intelligence, also referred to as machine learning and deep learning, allows a computer to quickly analyze massive amounts of information (data) and solve problems without human input. As analyst Brandon Purcell explains,

> AI is most helpful when the possible solution to a problem resides in large . . . datasets. If you think about climate data, there's a wealth of traditional structured data about temperature, sea levels, emissions levels, etc. But there's also a lot of unstructured data in the form of images, video, audio, and text. When it comes to analyzing massive amounts of unstructured data, deep learning is really the only game in town.[32]

The AI game is being played by some of the world's most advanced tech companies. Google uses its sophisticated AI network called DeepMind to analyze the company's energy consumption at its massive server farms. These large buildings hold an estimated 2.5 million computers that host the Google network. Server farms consume large amounts of electricity for power and cooling, but DeepMind was able to devise solutions that reduced energy consumption by 35 percent, cutting down on Google's $CO_2$ emissions. Likewise, the information gathered by DeepMind is being used for other energy-saving applications.

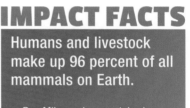

**IMPACT FACTS**

Humans and livestock make up 96 percent of all mammals on Earth.

—Ron Milo, environmental sciences professor

In Washington State, Microsoft is working with an environmental organization called Long Live the Kings, which is dedicated to restoring declining steelhead trout and king salmon populations. The organization is using AI to analyze data concerning fish and marine mammal movements, salmon and steelhead growth patterns, water pollution levels, and other conditions in the marine ecosystem. Artificial intelligence is creating models that are helping wildlife experts manage fish habitat, restore river ecology, and improve hatchery harvests.

Microsoft is also working with a group called Ocean Data Alliance to analyze biodiversity loss due to ocean acidification. As the name implies, Ocean Data Alliance gathers data from satellites and other sources concerning shipping, fishing, ocean mining, coral bleaching, and marine disease outbreaks. AI is helping the alliance slow the spread of invasive species, track plastic pollution, and monitor marine life. The data is being used in real time to help authorities predict problems and rapidly respond when problems occur.

The predictive power of AI is protecting endangered species such as rhinos, elephants, leopards, lions, and gorillas from poachers in wildlife sanctuaries in Asia, Africa, and elsewhere. An AI program called Protection Assistant for Wildlife Security (PAWS) crunches massive amounts of historical data to learn where illegal hunters have set snares and poached animals in the past. PAWS analyzes the locations of springs, rivers, and lakes where animals congregate, park roads used by poachers, and even the movements of endangered animals that are equipped with tracking devices. The program can identify poaching hot spots in huge wildlife sanctuaries where a few dozen park rangers are outmanned and outgunned by ruthless criminals who earn money poaching endangered animals.

PAWS produces maps with grids that allow rangers to schedule their patrols in areas that are at the highest risk for poaching. The program also applies what is called intelligent randomization. This helps rangers plan unpredictable patrol routes so poachers cannot anticipate their movements. Computer scientist Bistra Dilkina, who works with PAWS, predicts that the program will soon be in widespread use. "We could be in 600 protected areas around the world in more than 55 countries," Dilkina says. "That would really put PAWS at the forefront of the movement to fight poaching on a global scale."[33]

PAWS is part of a vast collective effort to roll back threats to biodiversity. Although humanity has never faced a crisis on this scale, people have never been better equipped to solve the problems being caused by climate change. In the modern, interconnected world, concerned citizens can organize online, study problems that are happening on other continents—or at bottom of the ocean—and use the latest high-tech advances to address problems beyond human understanding. While the battle against biodiversity loss can leave people feeling helpless and hopeless, raising a voice and fighting for a cause can be empowering. And as Thunberg says, inaction is not an option: "We can't just continue living as if there was no tomorrow, because there is a tomorrow."[34]

### Introduction: The War on Nature

1. Paul J. Crutzen and Christian Schwägerl, "Living in the Anthropocene: Toward a New Global Ethos," *Yale Environment 360*, January 24, 2011. https://e360.yale.edu.
2. Quoted in Census of Marine Life, "How Many Species on Earth? About 8.7 Million, New Estimate Says," ScienceDaily, August 24, 2011. www.sciencedaily.com.
3. Quoted Joanna Walters, "Greta Thunberg Tells Trump to 'Listen to the Science' After Arriving in New York," *The Guardian*, August 29, 2019. www.theguardian.com.

### Chapter One: What Is Biodiversity?

4. Quoted in Louis Bergeron, "Discovering Mammals Cause for Worry," *Stanford Report,* Stanford News, February 9, 2009. https://news.stanford.edu.
5. Quoted in Bergeron, "Discovering Mammals Cause for Worry."
6. Quoted in Rachel E. Gross, "The Moral Cost of Cats," *Smithsonian*, September 20, 2016. www.smithsonianmag.com.
7. Quoted in Elizabeth Kolbert, *The Sixth Extinction: An Unnatural History*. New York: Henry Holt, 2014, p. 162.
8. World Heritage Centre, "Manú National Park," United Nations Educational, Scientific and Cultural Organization. https://whc.unesco.org.
9. Quoted in Richard Grant, "Do Trees Talk to Each Other?," *Smithsonian*, March 2018. www.smithsonianmag.com.
10. Quoted in Grant, "Do Trees Talk to Each Other?"
11. Peter Wohlleben, *The Hidden Life of Trees: What They Feel, How They Communicate: Discoveries from a Secret World*. Vancouver, BC: Greystone Books, 2015, pp. 11–12.
12. Quoted in Bergeron, "Discovering Mammals Cause for Worry."

### Chapter Two: Hostile Invaders

13. Quoted in Aristos Georgiou, "U.S. National Parks Under 'Deep and Immediate Threat' from Feral Cats, Hogs, Rats,

and Other Invasive Species," *Newsweek*, December 6, 2019. www.newsweek.com.

14. Bill Finch, "The True Story of Kudzu, the Vine That Never Truly Ate the South," *Smithsonian*, September 2015. www.smithsonianmag.com.

15. Quoted in Phil Mercer, "The Rapid Spread of Australia's Cane Toad Pests," BBC News, March 22, 2017. www.bbc.com.

## Chapter Three: Forests Fall, Diversity Shrinks

16. Quoted in Colleen Walsh, "Amazon Blazes Could Speed Climate Change," *Harvard Gazette,* August 28, 2019. http://news.harvard.edu.

17. Quoted in Walsh, "Amazon Blazes Could Speed Climate Change."

18. Quoted in Carl Zimmer, "Birds Are Vanishing from North America," *New York Times,* September 19, 2019. www.nytimes.com.

19. Quoted in Google Arts & Culture, "Manual of Yanomami Traditional Medicine," 2016. https://artsandculture.google.com.

## Chapter Four: Threats to Ocean Ecosystems

20. Quoted in Dan Stillman, "Oceans: The Great Unknown," NASA, October 8, 2009. www.nasa.gov.

21. Quoted in Brad Plumer, "The Unprecedented Coral Bleaching Disaster at the Great Barrier Reef, Explained," Vox, March 31, 2016. www.vox.com.

22. Quoted in Mike Williams, "Gulf Coast Corals Face Catastrophe," Rice University News and Media Relations, Office of Public Affairs, December 5, 2019. www.news.rice.edu.

23. Quoted in Darryl Fears, "California Has a Weird New Desert. It's in the Pacific Ocean," *Washington Post,* February 1, 2019. www.washingtonpost.com.

24. Quoted in Stillman, "Oceans."

## Chapter Five: Addressing Problems, Reducing Threats

25. Quoted in Carline Harrap, "Greta Thunberg's Dad: How Fighting for the Climate Changed My Daughter," The Local, December 19, 2019. www.thelocal.se.

26. Quoted in Charlotte Alter, Suyin Haynes, and Justin Worland, "*Time* 2019 Person of the Year Greta Thunberg," *Time,* December 23–30, 2019. https://time.com.

27. Jamie Margolin, "Jamie Margolin's 2019 Congressional Testimony," House of Representatives, September 18, 2019. https://docs.house.gov/meetings/FA/FA14/20190918/109951/HHRG-116-FA14-Wstate-MargolinJ-20190918.pdf.

28. Quoted in Liz Kalaugher, "Climate Scientist or Climate Activist—Where's the Line?," Physics World, September 20, 2019. https://physicsworld.com.

29. Quoted in Burt Helm, "A Lot of Companies Want to Save the World. Impossible Foods Just Might Do It with Its Plant-Based Meats," *Inc.,* December 2019. www.inc.com.

30. Kierán Suckling, "Center for Biological Diversity Endorses Impossible, Beyond Burgers," Center for Biological Diversity, December 11, 2019. https://biologicaldiversity.org.

31. Quoted in Alessandro du Besse, "Drones Planting Trees: An Interview with BioCarbon Engineering," Impakter, May 7, 2019. https://impakter.com.

32. Quoted in Alison DeNisco Rayome, "How AI Could Save the Environment," TechRepublic, April 19, 2019. www.techrepublic.com.

33. Quoted in Marc Ballon, "Predictive AI Is the Newest Weapon in the Battle to Protect Endangered Animals," Phys.org, June 19, 2019. https://phys.org.

34. Quoted in Alter, Haynes, and Worland, "*Time* 2019 Person of the Year Greta Thunberg."

**1.** Join an environmental organization that is focused on biodiversity loss and climate change.

**2.** Register to vote when you turn eighteen and support leaders who promise to address important issues like biodiversity loss and climate change.

**3.** Eat less meat, especially beef, the production of which creates greenhouse gas emissions equal to all the cars, trucks, and airplanes worldwide.

**4.** If you eat seafood, learn which types are sustainable.

**5.** Avoid foods, shampoos, and makeup that lists palm oil as an ingredient.

**6.** Use energy wisely; turn off unused lights and electronics.

**7.** Walk, ride a bike, skateboard, or use public transportation when you travel.

**8.** Buy fewer clothes, gadgets, and other consumer goods; manufacturing contributes to climate change and biodiversity loss.

**9.** Join in a community garden project and plant trees.

**Alliance for Zero Extinction**—https://zeroextinction.org

The Alliance for Zero Extinction is composed of more than one hundred biodiversity conservation organizations working together to prevent species extinction by identifying and safeguarding habitat where endangered species live.

**BirdLife International**—www.birdlife.org

BirdLife International works with conservation organizations across the globe to conserve birds, save habitat, and ensure biodiversity. The group publishes an annual report that assesses the conditions of various ecosystems and tracks changes in bird populations.

**Center for Biological Diversity**—https://biologicaldiversity.org

The Center for Biological Diversity is one of the leading environmental organizations focused on saving threatened species and preventing extinction. The center's website contains a wealth of information about steps people can take to save endangered animals.

**Earth Guardians**—www.earthguardians.org

Earth Guardians is a student organization made up of activists, artists, and musicians dedicated to empowering young people to take over as leaders of the environmental movement. The group's website features comprehensive information about environmental issues and ongoing campaigns.

**NASA Earth Observatory**—https://earthobservatory.nasa.gov

This US space agency website features time-lapse satellite maps that show environmental changes over time in the Amazon rain forest, the Sierra Nevada, and elsewhere.

## Natural Resources Defense Council (NRDC)—www.nrdc.org

With more than 3 million members, the NRDC is one of the leading environmental organizations in the world. The council's website provides wide-ranging environmental information about climate change, biodiversity, forests, and oceans.

## North American Bird Conservation Initiative (NABCI)
http://nabci-us.org

This organization was founded to protect bird species that travel migration paths between the United States, Canada, and Mexico. NABCI monitors bird populations and produces reports meant to inform politicians and the public about threats to birds due to biodiversity loss.

## World Wildlife Fund (WWF)—www.worldwildlife.org

The WWF works to preserve wilderness, reduce threats to biodiversity, and stop pollution and climate change. As the world's largest environmental organization, the WWF supports around thirteen hundred conservation projects in one hundred countries.

### Books

Harriet Dyer, *The Little Book of Going Green: Really Understand Climate Change, Use Greener Products, Adopt a Tree, Save Water, and Much More!* New York: Skyhorse, 2019.

Lisa Idzikowski, *Biodiversity and Conservation*. New York: Greenhaven, 2019.

Stuart A. Kallen, *Trashing the Planet.* Minneapolis: Twenty-First Century Books, 2017.

Jennifer Swanson, *Geoengineering Earth's Climate: Resetting the Thermostat.* Minneapolis: Twenty-First Century Books, 2017.

Greta Thunberg, *No One Is Too Small to Make a Difference.* New York: Penguin, 2019.

### Internet Sources

Charlotte Alter, Suyin Haynes, and Justin Worland, "*Time* 2019 Person of the Year Greta Thunberg," *Time,* December 23–30, 2019. https://time.com.

Bob Berwyn, "In Australia's Burning Forests, Signs We've Passed a Global Warming Tipping Point," InsideClimate News, January 8, 2020. https://insideclimatenews.org.

Karin Brulliard, "North America Has Lost 3 Billion Birds in 50 Years," *Washington Post,* September 19, 2019. www.washingtonpost.com.

Rhett A. Butler, "2019: The Year Rainforests Burned," Mongabay, December 27, 2019. https://news.mongabay.com.

Darryl Fears, "California Has a Weird New Desert. It's in the Pacific Ocean," *Washington Post,* February 1, 2019. www.washingtonpost.com.

Anna Fletcher, "In Pictures: Invasive Species Around the World," CNN Travel, December 19, 2019. www.cnn.com.

Aristos Georgiou, "U.S. National Parks Under 'Deep and Immediate Threat' from Feral Cats, Hogs, Rats, and Other Invasive Species," *Newsweek,* December 6, 2019. www.newsweek.com.

Richard Grant, "Do Trees Talk to Each Other?," *Smithsonian,* March 2018. www.smithsonianmag.com.

Adam Zewe, "Artificial Intelligence Helps Rangers Protect Endangered Species," Phys.org, October 11, 2019. https://phys.org.

# Index

*Note: Boldface page numbers indicate illustrations.*

shipping, biological invasions
and, 28, 29
Simberloff, Daniel, 12
slash-and-burn agriculture,
33–34
Soil Conservation Service, 24
soil (pedosphere)
biodiversity in, 14–16
categories of biodiversity in,
15
in deserts, 18
feedback between plants
and, 16
mycorrhizal networks in,
16–18
Sosdian, Sindia, 44
Soto, Hernando de, 25
species
distribution of, 12
extinct, as percentage of all
species ever living on earth,
12
numbers existing on earth,
8–9
percentage classified of plant
*vs.* soil, 16
role in biodiversity of nature,
10
threatened by palm oil
production, 39

starfish, 50–51
Suckling, Kierán, 60, 61
sunflower sea star, 50–51

Taylor, Matthew, 55
Thunberg, Greta, 9, 54, **55**,
56, 65

United Nations, 7, 13, 14, 37,
51

wetlands, **8**
livestock production and
pollution of, 37
percentage lost to
development, 6
Wildlife Conservation Society,
36
Wohlleben, Peter, 16, 18
wood mouse, **11**
World Wildlife Fund (WWF),
71

Yanomami, Davi Kopenawa,
42
Yanomami people, 32–34, **34**,
40
yellow fever, 31

Zika virus, 31

Cover: FloridaStock/Shutterstock.com

8: Tom Camp/Shutterstock.com
11: Rudmer Zwerver/Shutterstock.com
13: Martin Mecnarowsky/Shutterstock.com
19: John D Sirlin/Shutterstock.com
22: ShyLama Productions/Shutterstock.com
26: Msnider/Shutterstock.com
30: InsectWorld/Shutterstock.com
34: Associated Press
38: First Resources/Shutterstock.com
41: John L. Absher/Shutterstock.com
45: I. Noyan Yilmaz/Shutterstock.com
48: Darkydoors/Shutterstock.com
52: RelentlessImages/Shutterstock.com
55: lev radin/Shutterstock.com
57: Kevin J. Frost/Shutterstock.com
64: Associated Press

Stuart A. Kallen is the author of more than 350 nonfiction books for children and young adults. He has written on topics ranging from the theory of relativity to the art of electronic dance music. In 2018 Kallen won a Green Earth Book Award from the Nature Generation environmental organization for his book *Trashing the Planet: Examining the Global Garbage Glut*. In his spare time, he is a singer, songwriter, and guitarist in San Diego.